# TO THE HOBO

## And Other Stories

## Ken Regan

WESTBOW
PRESS®
A DIVISION OF THOMAS NELSON
& ZONDERVAN

WestBow Press books may be ordered through booksellers or by contacting:

WestBow Press
A Division of Thomas Nelson & Zondervan
1663 Liberty Drive
Bloomington, IN 47403
www.westbowpress.com
1 (866) 928-1240

ISBN: 978-1-9736-5872-6 (sc)
ISBN: 978-1-9736-5873-3 (hc)
ISBN: 978-1-9736-5871-9 (e)

Library of Congress Control Number: 2019904061

Print information available on the last page.

WestBow Press rev. date:  04/05/2019

# Prologue

Help the hobo while he stands.
You know his problem,
but do you understand?
          Oklahoma -
he'll be there in the morning.
          Oklahoma -
tonight he'll be gone.

# Mister Perdi is Awake

There's a shuffling of feet next door,
Mr. Perdi is awake.
Soon he'll reach his mirror,
let the water run as he comes alive.
Mr. Perdi will have his coffee,
the morning paper may be read.
Mr. Perdi will go out;
but where will he go?
No job, no family, no friends to speak -
Mr. Perdi will walk the streets.

Evening will come,
I'll be glad to be back home;
rest from work and daytime's rush -
nighttime reserved for friends.

Keys will jangle, and may be dropped;
Mr. Perdi enters the room next door.
His TV will be too loud,
but he'll be asleep before I get back in.

Tomorrow I'll arise all too early
to start my life again.

There'll be a shuffling of feet next door;
Mr. Perdi is awake -
but where will he go?
Where will he go?

# To The Squirrel Who Shared My Dinner

The older ones ran away,
but not you, my little friend.
I guess you were too young to know
Man is to be feared.
Instinct should have told you
Danger - Man - Beware.

But you were hungry,
and I had food to spare.
Cool autumn winds signaled winter's coming,
and as you chewed happily - I wondered
how many more meals you'd be able to share.

Maybe it's indecent I should have so much
when you scrounge for each scrap.
But you ate in silence, uncomplaining,
glad for what you had.

When the time was over you scampered on your way.
I was glad for the moment of friendship,
but now it leaves me scared.
My wide eyed little friend, so trusting unafraid
will the next person you meet teach you, too late
that Man is to be feared?

# An M.D. Is Never Wrong

"I'm afraid you're dead."
is what the doctor said.

"How could that be,
I feel all right to me."

"Be that as it may,
I declare your death today."

"Doctor, if you please
give my wrist a squeeze.
Can't you hear my heart;
Doctor, you've given me a start.
Please check your book,
Doctor, take another look."

"I won't change my mind
on what I decide.
Take a look, you'll find
you've already died."

# The Cosmos Are Caving In On This Sunny Sunday Afternoon

It's a sunny Sunday afternoon.
Birds sing, children play.
Mrs. Hardwick's having a tea.

Somewhere over the hill
the cosmos are caving in.
The train arrives at ten.

Laughter in the park,
the bells chime in.
Everyone's agreed, such a lovely day.
Packing for your journey,
clothes squeezed in,
leaving no room for memories.

Sunny Sunday
under my bed
waiting for the cosmos to cave in.
Your train arrives at ten.

# Captain Cornfield

Captain Cornfield
Seaman, strong and wise.
Forty two years from ship to ship,
all the world passed before his eyes.

Through storm and winds
his cargo he delivered.
The men feared no sea monsters
for Captain Cornfield was at the helm.

Captain Cornfield
Seaman, tried and true.
Forty two years from sea to sea,
and nothing he could not do.

Every vessel at times must port,
the men rush to land in childlike expectation.
Alone in his cabin Captain Cornfield would sit,
studying maps and charts.

Captain Cornfield
Seaman, until the end.
Forty two years from life to life,
with the sea his only friend.

# May Day

An unassuming day on the fifth of May
I was happy going along as I was.
You came along with your song
pretending to be another side of me.

A wonderful girl, one in the world
I fell into your spell.

A sunny day on the eighth of May
You had all the love I could give.

Surprise of wonders, the joys of lovers.
I checked under the covers, you were gone.

Just another day on this twelfth of May
I'm sitting here all alone.

I was happy before you,
happy with you, without you I am blue.

There'll be another day, come some May
I will have you out of my mind
Flowers will be blooming, I'll be sitting unassuming,
I will hear another song.
But on that day I'll remember last May
I will hum my own tune then.

# To The Hobo

I was a child of the fifties,
born just in time to see you die.
But I remember, something
beyond explaining.
      A feeling
of the freedom

we might have shared.

You are the Hobo,
a free soul by name,
your destiny is what you make it.

I seek to follow,
but the trail is lost.

To the Hobo,
wherever you may be:
come out from your hiding
and return to me.

# A Simple Little Café

It was a simple little café
that opened up each day at three.
Gilda owned the key, the bank owned the rest.
She did her best to make a buck each day.
After twenty years all she had was me.
Only I withstood the test.

Gilda cried the day she said goodbye
to it all. Gilda, my friend,
you're at the end of the road.

It was a simple little café
that was boarded up yesterday.
Gilda kept the key, the bank took the rest.
She's getting too old, that's what they all said.
After twenty years only I remained.
Only I withstood the test.

And when she died
only I stood by the grave,
as they lay her to rest
clutching a key to her breast.

Gilda cried the day she said goodbye
to it all. Gilda, my friend,
you've reached the end of the road.

# A Question of Priorities

Frederick was over, past the line.
Brought too far by a misguided rage.

Momma cried, though she did not understand.
"Our boy's a precious gem, he's far too kind."

Mrs. Harkins down the street disagrees,
She's seen him in his worser days.

Frederick seemed all the talk about the town.
Meanwhile, a little girl rests untimely in her grave.

# Two Rocking Chairs

Two rocking chairs.
One moving mechanically
back to front,
front to back,
back to front.

The other silent
with the night.

One old man,
living mechanically
night to day,
day to night,
night to day.

# A Journeyman's Son

A Journeyman's son
with no home of his own;
he sat on the border,
he traveled alone.
Sometimes facing west,
often looking east;
searching for something
kept just out of reach.

A Journeyman's son
sitting under a broken moon;
hoping for salvation,
walking toward the sun.
Stopping, going
it's all the same.
Summer turns to fall,
the path continues to go on.

# Casualty

It wasn't his war;
he was no soldier.
He missed the laugh
tossed casually off her shoulder.

She played games
like the world was on fire.
To her it was no crime
to play the part of the liar.

It wasn't his war,
but he paid the price.
She let him go
with the toss of the dice.

# This Sacred Ground

"Dearly Beloved,"
the preacher said,
"we are gathered here
to give thanks."

But as I look down
on the cold hard ground
I can only hear
the cries of shame.

"The brave have fought,"
but it's the weak who die.
And no one standing here
can answer why.

"This sacred ground,"
his are hollow words.
One brother's cause is now
one brother's loss.

# Steam Train Maury, Frisco Jack, T-Bone Slim

You're Alive!
Hallelujah!
Praise the Lord!

I first heard it on the late night news -
The Hobo's back in town.
The King came riding the rails.

My heart stopped a bit
to allow a tear to form,
crossing my face
in silent memoriam.

Ah, but your numbers are few
and dwindling evermore.
From thousands to a busload.
Your days are growing short.

And when the last of you
is buried in the ground
my heart will stop once more
and the tears will flow in thousands
in silent memorial to each one of your kind.

# Too Good For You

"You're too good for me"
was all she said
before she walked out the door.
"I'm not good enough for you"
she said to me
as she walked out of my life.

"You're too good for me"
is all they ever say
as they leave me with my tears.
Funny,
when you're too good for everyone
you're not good enough for anyone.

# Sitting In A Capsule

Sitting in a capsule
waiting for the countdown to begin
he thinks about his life
and where it will end.

Down below
technicians run
through thousands of equations,
double checking each one
to make sure that they've got it right.

Staring at the dials
his mind begins to wander,
and he begins to wonder
where it is he's going to.

But now is not the time
to think about such things,
for the countdown has started;
time to get into routine.

Ten seconds left and counting,
Major Harris, best of luck to you.
It's a shame your wife wasn't here to see you,
but I'm sure she had something else to do.

Three, two, one and zero.
The rocket streaks toward heaven,
passing it up for the stars.

Down on earth
ten thousand cheer.
Up in space
he sits alone.

And his mind begins to wander;
Yes, and he begins to wonder
where it is he's going to
and where the years have brought him.

Down on earth
all NASA cries
Major Harris, what have you done?
You've severed communications
and let loose all your earthly ties.

Millions of dollars in equipment,
years of planning
all gone to waste
because in this day of sophistication
one man could not hang onto his wife.

# The Oldest Living Relative of Someone Long Since Dead

He was the oldest living relative of someone long since dead
looking out at all the world, seeing inside his head.
Telegraphs and telephones, communications jammed
he smiled with a knowing eye, the future wasn't always planned.
He seemed to me a solitary man, I knew him as a friend.
Hiding in a covered box, searching for the key
he was the oldest living relative of someone long since dead.

I never asked him questions, I knew what he would have said:
The old man, he never talked too much, he was a mystic
but he was not God. The ages were not kind to him,
he folded his wings and died.
He left me, a son, to carry on the game.
But seeing this world today, somehow it's not the same.

He was the oldest living relative of someone long since dead
fighting to be himself, not a prophet to be led.
He followed his father's ways of a time no longer held dear
the ages were not kind to him, he folded his wings and died.

# Lady Samantha

Lady Samantha
had the best of everything;
breakfast in bed,
brunch on the balcony.
Lady Samantha
could have the best of anything;
and it's true what they've said,
that she once had me.

I was a boy,
she needed some fun.
Her long blonde hair
kept me playing her game.

When she was tired of her toy
she sent me on the run.
I pretended I didn't care,
but she hurt me all the same.

Lady Samantha
had the best of everything;
but she wanted her cake
and she wanted to eat it too.

Lady Samantha
you can't have everything.
The next time you awake
I won't be there with you.

# The Early Train

Are you far away?
Can you hear me calling?
Do you still miss me?

It was a misty Sunday morning,
the sun decided not to show.
She took the early train for the east;
My love, where did you go?

Are you far away?
Can you hear me calling?
Do you still miss me?

Now I listen to the quiet breeze
blowing gently westward;
waiting for a sign saying
she's returning home to me.

Standing upon the mountain tops
looking for something I cannot see;
calling into the echoing valleys
wondering if she can hear me.

Are you far away?
Can you hear me calling?
Did you ever love me?

# Useless Gifts

A broken heart,
two china cups
and a picture of you.

That's all you gave to me;
none do me any good,
as I've run out of tea.

# Good For Nothing

Diamond ring
meant for you
good for nothing,
save for cutting glass.
I'm cutting glass.

# Nothing Grows Forever

The rains came slowly, as the fires gave way;
when it was over, the forest was burnt to the ground.

Dear Emily, I remember the seed we planted,
we were children of not too many years.
We made a promise that as long as that tree grew
we would be together, me and you.

The men who fought the flames were too tired
to place the blame; a careless match
had burned the forest down.

Emily, I would have married you;
I believed in children's dreams.
You left me without a reason why,
our love you simply outgrew.

They returned to their beds for a rest
with tears in their eyes of something precious lost.

What a shame nothing stays the same;
something's gone that can never be replaced.
Why does it happen, no one knows:
People shrug, saying nothing grows forever.

Dear Emily, the last reminder's gone;
you broke the promise, I burned the dream to the ground.

What a shame nothing stays the same;
something's gone that can never be replaced.
Why does it happen, no one knows:
People shrug, saying nothing grows forever.

# In Memoriam

You're born in the world,
expected to be what
they want you to be.

But you, you had to
be you.
You, you're breaking
all the rules.

The machinery men
tried to strap you down.
The white-wash fools
chased you from town
to town.

But you, you had to be
free.

You're a one of a kind,
a non-surviving breed.
The factory men
won't let you breathe.
You bleed, but they
won't accept it as real.

You're born in the world,
expected to be.

But you, you had to
set yourself free.

# I Bombed Pearl Harbor

I admit,
it was all my fault.
The blame is mine.
I was the one who never tried.
It was me that let the love die.
I was the one who left you.
Oh, and I bombed Pearl Harbor too.

Make it easy on yourself,
don't take on any of the blame.
Push it all on me.
Anything to ease your mind
and forget how you hurt me.

The pain I feel, I did to myself.
I made all the mistakes.
I brought the rain that gave you a cold.
I caused your car to crash,
though I was a thousand miles away.
I broke your stereo.
I was Mrs. O'Leary's cow.
I take the blame for Waterloo.
And of course, I bombed Pearl Harbor too.

# Question

Going into Brighton.
I heard his sad cry
"We are all bleeders,
why do some not die?"

There was anguish or terror
passing through him inside.
I tried to reach to him,
but my hand only died.
I hid in my paper,
dreamed of Lily and tea,
but his heart kept pounding
'til it beat over me.
"You look cold and hungry,
somewhat less than satisfied;
is there something I can do for you,
do you need a friend to confide?"

He looked at me slowly,
then he started to cry.
But he would not speak to me,
he just kept repeating
"Why do some not die?
Why do some not die?"

"I don't know what you mean, sir;
could you be more clear.
I would like to help you,
if you need me, I'm here."

Over and over he would only say
"We are all bleeders,
why do some not die?"

Finally, he looked up
then told me his name.
"I am Jim Hanner,
my wife was Janine.
She was an actress,
she played my part;
she died last Tuesday,
taking my heart."

"I see that you're grieving."
I said, breaking in:
"Yes, we're all bleeders,
but we've got to go on."

He stopped me soundly
with only one word
"You say go on sir,
I say
WHY?"

I had not an answer,
though many flashed past.
I could not find one
with meaning to last.
I got off the bus,
it was my stop;
I left him alone
to be with my own love at home.

Lily was waiting with a hot cup of tea.
She went to hug me, I held her tight.
Then I told her about the man I'd met that night.
She said it was sad how lonely he was,
then she turned on the TV.
I went outside.
Looking up to the stars,
to the heavens I cried
"We are all bleeders,
why do some not die?"

# Birds of Flight

Someone cried,
I heard it in the sunrise.
A sad goodbye,
the plane is in the air.

Every day
there's a jet leaving
into the sun,
someone's left alone.

Birds of flight,
iron cannot cry.
What gives you the right
to take away one's own?

# We're Going To War, Amy

### I

We're going to war, Amy.
Pack up my bags, I'm
on my way.

War is man's work, Amy.
I'm off to join with
the boys.

For glory, pride, and honor
Amy, I must not delay.
Kiss me now, my love
I'll be home soon.

### II

Men are so stupid,
never growing out of
children's games.

Why is man's work to get
slaughtered, leaving widows home
to pray?

For glory, pride, and honor
words have no meaning
when one is left to cry
over the grave.

# The Last Dance of GEDji and Maen

Stars in tune, dance of the lights:
two lovers rapt in the night.
GEDji was calm, Maen walked on;
windswept ocean holding the moon.

It was dream, it was real;
one last time for fairies to feel.

Flames beat the dark, 'til light beat the flames;
urgency maddened the pace of the game.
Maen looked down, GEDji passed on:
more t han one tear for magic now gone.

Stars sometime twinkle bright in the sky,
some say Maen slowly glides by.

# They Say She Dances

They say she dances.
Though she came inside
soon she would glide
right past the fences.
They say she dances.

All alone, on my own
she waltzed right past me.
I didn't know then
I would meet her again
and we would tango.
Oh how she dances.

Her name was June
and soon she was in me
- hopping through me.

They say she dances.
Though she came inside
soon she would glide
right past the fences.
They say she dances.

Came the end of May,
then the day she rose to fullness
and left me holding.

I sway solitaire,
but someday I swear
she'll hear the music:
We all take our chances.

They say she dances.

# Deja Vu

Deja Vu
the quiet child looks at you.
He's seen it all before,
a parent walking out the door.
Tell him not to cry,
try to explain why
endings must come.
Love is for some,
but not you.
Deja Vu

# Hand-Grenade

It was like a hand-grenade
breaking against the night.
Your words ripped across my chest,
tearing a gash left opened wide.

It's moved on again,
this restless heart.
Where next it surfaces
bound loosely at my side
I can only wonder.
I only know the pin will once more be pulled,
like a hand-grenade breaking against the night.

# Her Silent Room

She knows no laughter
in her silent room.
No walls of wonder,
only doubt and gloom.

She keeps no pictures
to give her life;
only facts and figures
cut through like a knife.

She was a dancer
on a golden stage.
Bright lights of wonder
gave way to age.

She holds no reason
for going on.
She contemplates tomorrow,
wishing it were done.

# Seeds

A spiritual war was being waged,
less good against more bad.
Angels lined on either side
to see who would survive.
Demons laughed as their numbers grew,
no victory for any but they.

Off far away a farmer sowed
seeds on a lonely plain.
One lowly beast to pull the plow,
one humble soul to till the future;
Against the hordes of hatred,
what hope was one to find?

# The Boardwalk Was Empty

The boardwalk was empty,
chased off by winded rains.
Blown off course perhaps,
one off season pro wandered in
and sat at the booth in the rear.

Music played on casually
filtered through the smoke.
Conversations mixed in and out,
his ear caught bits and phrases.
No word had he to offer
to the changing serenade;
three beers lasted into evening
when the closing call came.

He left the place aimlessly.
The boardwalk was empty
as the storm seaward called.
A single splash was swallowed
in the pounding of the shore.
Any words spoken would go unheard,
the boardwalk was empty.

# The Warring Tribe

The Madness has begun.
A drumbeat gains momentum;
the call is made.

Hiding in the jungle,
two lovers take to flight.
Seeking to escape the carnage,
they hide their faces in the ground.

Across the Atlantic
reports begin to blur
into a cacophony of misinformation.
The cameras turn their focus
upon the Warring Tribe.

Amid the bombs flying overhead
a child is born.
The two lovers lift their heads.
There is a cause
Something worth more
than tribal squabbles;
a thing of more value
than border lines.
The two lovers turn toward the town
to give themselves in battle of a higher kind.

# The Morning After

I met you on the morning after.
You were sitting at the bus depot.
There was sadness in your eyes that morning,
a sadness that I've known myself.
I took you home on the morning after.
You became a part of my life.
There was happiness in my soul shining,
a shining I'd not had before.

Now here I am on the morning after.
You packed your bags and took my heart.
I've lived through too many morning's after,
you'd think by now I'd sleep in late.

# Vagabond Song

Looking toward the sunrise,
heading for tomorrow.
I must keep moving on
like a Vagabond.

If I had wings to fly
I'd be there by and by.
As it is I keep going on
like a Vagabond.

All across the country,
stretching from sea to sea.
Direction unknown,
I'm just a Vagabond.

If I had wings to fly
I know I'd get there by an
As it is I keep moving o
like a Vagabond.

# Life Sentence

She never had her way,
someone always ran the show.
Fantasy stepped in
and gave her control;
in her dreams she ruled.
She set out to make them real.

He never stood a chance,
her strength was in her hands.
Reality hit too hard
and ended his world.
In her dreams she ruled.
She finally had her way.

# Sent Sailing

She sent him sailing
on lakes mirroring the sun.
She let him wander
'til his wandering was done.

He made his journeys
running swiftly through his mind.
He never knew her;
she thought she was being kind.

# The Ledge

Last night we stood on a ledge
staring at the edge of devotion.
Somebody said, "You're better off dead
than surviving on pent up emotion".

As summer's night grew dark
we fled to a park
hoping to find some direction.
But the storms blew in
and before we could begin
someone showed us our severed connection.

So before the dawn you packed your bags
as I waited for sunlight's embrace.
But the warmth never came
as I stood in the rain
taking in my own reflection.

# Frozen Image

Are you going to the store?
Could you buy me a picture frame?
    I have a photo
    I want to capture
    on display
    for all to see.

    Behind the glass
    is the image
    I want to keep.
The one of me and you
    in younger days.
Smiles upon our faces,
happiness shining through.

Are you going to the store?
Could you buy me a picture frame?
    One to replace
the broken glass upon the floor.
    I need to recapture
    a moment
long since gone from view.

# Without a Clue

He sat in on the world's games
tossing the dice on his turn.
Changing the rules was his favorite thing,
keeping us from catching up
or catching on.
We sit on boards without a clue
moving back and forth
at another's whim.
He controls the plays.
Even the other gods play along
without a clue.

# Child at the Station

Child at the station
wandering through life;
passengers embarking,
she sees not the train.

Child at the station,
the world passes through.
You see none of it,
but neither do they see you.

# Alexandra Walks the Nile

Alexandra walks the Nile,
as below the water I watch
unable to breathe for the beauty
     floating above.

Alexandra smiles, as nervously
she covers her face.
Inside my heart I melt away;
no work of art created by man
could capture the look
that leaps across my dreams.

Alexandra holds a key;
if she only knew the power therein.
Would she hold it within
keeping me dangling as I do now,
or would she unlock the feelings
that too long have gone untouched?

# Safety in Nothing
# (The Dilemma of Non-Existence)

I journeyed down to the borderline,
the man on watch said not to cross.
"There's always trouble on the other side,
stay where you are, where happiness lies."
I traveled up to the mountain peaks,
a wise man in a cave met me on top.
"Why have you come," he asked, annoyed;
"there's nothing up here that can't be seen
from the safety of your own home.

> Better to stay in bed
> than to count the stars;
> better to live in hope
> than cross over the edge."

I sat for days inside my house
watching the lawn cover up my view.
Claustrophobia has replaced my dream,
I need a scythe to escape this trap.

# When the Grimsby Comes to Town

Children speak in whispers
when the Grimsby comes to town.
Adults hide their purses
and turn the pictures down.

The Grimsby walks in silence,
smoke comes out his nose.
No one asks why he's there
because everybody knows.

The people made a promise
many years before;
anything was his to have
if the Grimsby'd stop the war.

With fearsome rage
and all his strength released
the Grimsby went to battle
to bring about a peace.

As the years went by
people walked without a care
'til the word went out
soon the Grimsby would be there.

The questions burned on all their lips,
What tribute would he desire?
Would he take their young away
or set the town on fire?

But this time seemed so different
his whole body seemed to creak;
he sat down in the corner square
as they listened to him speak.

"I've grown old and tired.
Long and far I've roamed.
Now I have but one request,
I want this to be my home."

In shocked surprise they heard him
as a tear came to his eye.
"Yes, Mr. Grimsby join us,
there's no cause for you to cry."

Now the children laugh and sing,
there's no reason to look down,
and everyone is happy
because the Grimsby's come to town.

# Hobo

Poor soul, they call you.
Misguided fool, from others less kind.
You are the hobo,
your fortune is in the wind,
a map of steel rails to lead you;
living for the day,
or for a better day yet to come.

Your number once was great
back in the old days,
the depression days.
You started out as bums:
men without a job,
without a home.

You grew in size,
until you were not alone.
You got a name for yourselves -
Hobos
the last in the line of kings.
You had dignity, sitting over the fire
cooking your can of beans.

Lonely nights under the stars,
lulled by the distant whistles
of tomorrow's ride.

But the better days came
(maybe not for you).
Your kind began dying out;
        the art was lost.

Today you still wander,
lost amid a world of ever-speeding time.
You walk among the flock of phonies,
        the dropouts from life
trying to imitate your free spirit.
        But you are not like them;
you worked hard at what you did.
You did not give up on society,
you survived it as only you could.

Your beginnings were a circumstance of time;
        and so came your diminishing.
But the times move in circular waves,
        and your day may return.
            Unemployment
may force the flower children off the streets,
and your numbers will again flourish.

        The hobo will return.
        But will we take notice
        of the unkempt tramp
        riding the rails?

# At My Door

At my door
a childhood dream
decided to check in.

Such innocence
and youthful verve
an energy barely contained.

It looked at me
and shed a tear,
then turned and walked away.

In its steps
a slowed down pace,
a lesser, weakened soul.

At my door
I stood, alone
feeling older than before.

# The Song I Knew

In a backward way
along a wooded walk
in a foreign land
by a bearded fool
a minstrel plays
another tune
from the one I knew.

The one I knew
was a sweeter sound
with softer strings
playing along in time;
no wasted words
behind each harmony,
no stranger's smile
staring back at me.

In another time
when the tune was ours
the way was clear
through the trees ahead;
the woods we knew
played a song or two,
the song I knew
was me and you.

# Missing Dimension

There is no motion
on a static shelf;
no hearts dancing
on a lifeless wall.

We're like a painting
nice to look at;
but one dimension
is no life at all.

# The Plain-Eye-See

Go to the mountain of the Plain-Eye-See.
They said better days waiting there for you, for me.
Go to the mountain before you visit the well.
A better moment growing, go and tell.
Across the border you will find a road
with a shack of Burdens to lay your load.
Proceed in freedom through a deep blue sea,
there you'll find the mountain of the Plain-Eye-See.
Climb the mountain of the Plain-Eye-See.
Climb for days so that you may be
a better person than you were before,
a better child, and a whole lot more.
Then at last you may drink of the well.
Be at rest, there's no more to tell.

# Legacy

Creation moves swiftly
across borders made by man.
Children learn the lessons
they pay for at our hands.
Tomorrow won't remember
who we were or why;
but tomorrow can't dismiss
the damage that was ours.

# The Tiger

In anger the tiger strikes,
yet there is beauty.
For I have known the softness,
the strength behind her eyes.

The tiger is a moment,
her precious touch the reality
fulfilling my dream.

# 24 Hours Behind the Wheel

It's been raining for days;
you're out there somewhere.
On the road, 24 hours behind the wheel;
there's no slowing down, always one more load.
If only you could stop your running
and turn around to face me;
It's been raining for days.

# Broken

Broken hearted child
in a broken world.
Broken pieces
surround your room,
broken dreams
caress your heart.

Broken hearted child
in a broken world.
Fancy clothes
on a plain design,
fancy plans
beyond your scope.

Broken hearted child
in a broken world.
Adulthood screams
when it comes too soon,
adulthood cries
when it's a little girl.

# Somewhere Else

It was just another Tuesday night,
#18 Train was late again.
I stood along a line
of faces all somewhere else.
I was back in Spain.

They were better days,
young hearts could take the strain
of changing loves, romantic nights
and days spent alone.

It was another world,
we led separate lives.
Explorers, survivors of the war.
Then we found each other,
sparks of passion playing
amid candle burning conversations.

Now it's a different time,
age has changed the dreams.
A home, three kids - "family".
We still lead separate lives
under the banner of togetherness.

Just another Tuesday night,
the train finally came - too soon.
Spain was held off for another time -
another line of faces all somewhere else.

# Actress

Broken hearted lady,
cry away your nights;
hiding beneath the spotlight,
no one sees beyond the play.

The crowds roar out approval,
a life lived on display;
discarded feelings lay open,
the stage's the thing, they say.

Yet, you had your dreams once,
but no one wrote the words.
You gestured in pantomime,
but no one heard the pain.

Broken hearted lady,
giving up a little more each night.
Morning will come,
late edition's reviews will rate your last goodbye.

# No Triangle

Two:
and a third,
No triangle -
Only pain
for one.

# Breakwater

In a hideaway
far from the main road
he sits on a back porch
watching the river run.
He lets his dreams flow by.

# Sheila

Sheila, sunrise
hurts my eyes.
Please close the shade.

This bed of mine
is my security,
won't you come join me.

Sheila, darling
you're my world;
Never leave this room.

It's my prison,
you're my jailer;
yes, you hold the key.

I feel the darkness
covering my eyes,
Sheila, close the shade.

# So You Tell Me (a Conversation)

So you tell me
it's just not working out for you.
So I ask you
do you know what you want?

I can't tell you,
let's just let it be.
I am hungry,
you're not feeding the need in me.

So you tell me,
but do you ever feel my pain?
It's not over
if we only try again.

Can't you see the truth,
there's nothing more of
what once was.
Let it go. Don't hold on.

So you tell me
it doesn't seem right to you.
Do you know
a better way to go?

# I've Heard Her Cry at Night

Why can't I help her?
I've heard her cry at night.
She moves through her day
smiling at those she sees.
Then she comes home.

Why can't I help her?
I've heard her cry at night.
Is she reaching out,
or only falling in?
She won't tell me.

Why can't I help her?
I've heard her cry at night.
She must walk alone
until she finds the one who's right,
I know it isn't me.

# Train Into the Night

Plied into submission,
an answer strains against the wind.
New light wearies of the burden,
another train disappears into the night.
Before the dawn
she'll have made her decision;
a lonely whistle
moves toward the horizon.

# The Back Row

From the back row
I see what's going on.
I watch others watching others,
from the back I see it all.

From the back row
I witness life going on.
Others interact,
from the back I sit alone.

# Play the Role

I've played the game
by the rules
they set for me.

You play the same game
with a different set of rules.
You break them all the same.

You win,
while I continue to lose.
The dice have been thrown,
I'll play the roll -
you sweep them into your pocket.

Victories you win,
but destroy the game.

# Stories & Truth

I never tried to write the story,
it came as a play within a play.
The words weren't mine,
though I wish they were;
I've tried to capture them,
but time won't let me.

In the scheme of things
it was not so great -
the attention surpassed the dream.

I've long since tried to redo the story,
one can't repeat what never was.
It never was mine,
though I wish it were;
the dream outlives the person,
the play becomes the dream.

# She's Going Home

Do you know where she's gone?
I left her so long ago
on the road.
Pushing products,
making contacts,
leaving friends;
the road wears you down.
She's on her way home.
She's going home.

Growing older,
getting gray,
still making a dollar
while losing friends.
It has a way of
tearing you down.

Do you know where she's gone?
I left her on the road
so long ago.
She's on her way home;
she's going home.

# Greed

Placed away on a mountain
far from prying eyes
an amulet from an angel
cast in gold, set in jewels
glowing brightly in sunshine,
holding its warmth by moonlight.

One day a stranger
getting away from the crowd
found the priceless wonder
and took it back to town.

The riches it promised
were his to have,
but he could not hold them
and he fled far away.

Placed in a window
for all to admire
an amulet from an angel
began its life on a shelf.

# Sing-Along

Sit not in silence
when the music calls for you.
Hear the chorus swelling
asking for an answer
somewhere amidst the tune.

Sit not in silence
while the singer sings his song.
Fill the room with rejoicing,
the singer asks you to sing along.

# (Something's Not Right)
# On Pleasant Avenue

There is a street called Pleasant Avenue.
Houses are big, yards are clean,
neighbors smile on Pleasant Avenue.
But inside the doors closed tight
another kind of world goes on;
something's not right on Pleasant Avenue.

Neighbors wave and say hello,
and they might even know your name,
but they never cross the line
into knowing who you are.
They don't want to know, so they ignore
something's not right on Pleasant Avenue.

Each shut into their private life,
but windows leak and let out truth;
angry voices are heard, things are broken,
children cry, carry bruises unspoken.
Things seem fine, but if one only knew,
something's not right on Pleasant Avenue.

# To The Hobo I Met By The Campfire

He came into town upon a railroad car,
a roving bull among the cows.
With all he had on his back and
in his living. He lived by his wits
and by the land God had given.

I met him one night by the campfire,
a roving bull among his own kind.
He said, "You have a good face,
the lines of life have not yet set in."
It was then he told me his story,
I tried my best to take it all in.

"I'm a dropout from the world,
but I've dropped into myself.
I've learned a lot about life,
but in the quest for knowledge
the road is always just beginning.

I can't tell you how to live,
I can't even show you what to find.
But I can tell you the words
that are always on my mind."

He said, "Living's free and easy,
if you're willing to pay the price.
I met an old man and took his advice:
'I'd rather die being me
than grow old and never know
what I was all about.'"

He laughed a bit at the memory,
and drew it in with a sigh.
"Maybe it makes no sense to you,
but it does to me. That's what counts."

I remembered that man
throughout my travels,
and told his story wherever I'd go.
It was sad when I'd heard he died
jumping a car in Memphis,
still a roving bull among cows.

But I remembered his words
and I smiled. He truly lived
to the end.

Each town, each mile,
each campfire I sit,
I gaze at the faces,
and to each lineless face I say,

"Living's free and easy,
if you're willing to pay the price.
I met an old man and took his advice:
'I'd rather die being me
than grow old and never know
what I was all about.'"

Maybe it makes no sense to you,
but it does to me. That's what counts.

# Actors

Last night I saw a play,
and watched the actors on the stage.
They knew their lines and played their parts,
but I didn't believe a word.
I've lived on stages
and played the parts,
I have laughed and I have cried.
I know the play is not the truth,
you can act, but you can't be real.

# In A Downtown Bar

By the time the police arrived
the damage was already done.
It wasn't his first time in the bar,
nor the first time he'd been drunk.
It was, though, his first bitter taste of love
and the first time he armed his gun.

In a booth in a downtown bar
the world can pass away.
Life is self-contained;
every day is different, yet the same.

# Fragile

The card said 'Don't Touch'
  but … ,

Fifty dollars for pieces
of glass on a linoleum floor.

# Contradiction

Spilling forth in controversy,
a bitter feud began.
Masked by sundry pleasantries
the fires grew inside
until blown apart in equity,
a frigid winter blew.

# Lady Enigma

She found her pleasure
in making overtures to the unknown.
She would not feast on candy,
only bite the head and hand
of opportunity.
Late, in songs of darkness,
she spun magic tales only she knew
to be real.
Mystical, some called her.
Only she knew the truth.

# Shallow Pools

I see in each star
a story too far to be told;
a depth too rich to hold
for one like me
who dreams in shallow pools
of water.

Shallow pools of madness
ripple as the stone is cast;
her heart so deep and fast
could not be contained
in such shallow pools of rain.

I hear in each story
a message beyond my grasp;
far beyond a narrow gasp
from my tortured brain -
everything sounds the same
inside shallow pools of water.

# The Border Guard

When nighttime comes
out of hiding they creep;
seeking freedom,
looking to start anew.
Their chance will never come;
no one gets by the Border Guard.

# The Candle

When the flame burned down the candle wax
until at last it had smothered itself in its own destruction
I realized the love affair was through.
We tried; lighting new matches when the fire went out.
But now there is no wick, nor wax enough to build anew;
all is darkness - for me and for you.

# The Plains of Pride

They were divided on the question of unity.
So they took their stands on either side.
Steadfast in their positions,
not yielding to compromise:
we buried all the bodies together
on the plains of pride.

# Throwaways

They were throwaways,
junk on the table
in a garage somewhere forgotten.
Left by time,
deemed no longer useful
sitting in a rocking chair
in some Home somewhere forgotten.

# (If I Write A Song)
# Would You Be My Lyric?

Someday, if I write a song
would you be my lyric?
I'd need a melody,
would your love flow to me?

Music is never right without the rhyme;
Half a love can waste your time.
Someday if I write a song
would you be my lyric?

# Melinda Never Cried

Melinda sometimes smiled
as she passed through your heart.
She said she could not be tied down,
but she was sorry just the same.
Though she said she'd be sad
I saw her smile as she said goodbye.
Melinda sometimes smiled,
but she never cried.

# A Tragedy

It's a tragedy -
a life gone to waste,
a love washed away in tears.
It's a tragedy.

It's a comedy -
a fool wasting time
trying to bring it together.
It's a comedy.

It's just my life -
not a play for you to watch,
not worth the price of admission.
It's just my life.

# "By The Way, She Married This May"

It came in a letter from home,
"by the way, she married this May."
I remember when you'd write me,
promising to wait forever;
forever ended on that page
"by the way, she married this May."

When I think of the years wasted
planning all my life around you
it makes me wish that time would stop
so that I could reform my life.
It's too late to change, I move on.
It came in a letter from home,
"by the way, she married this May."

I wish you well, though you dropped me,
it's your life to do as you will:
in the end, you reap what you sow.
It's you and he together now,
while I am left out in the cold.
I'm entering Year One, thanks to
"by the way, she married this May."

# Old Bessie

The fever hit old Bessie McGree,
took her life at eighty-three.
The funeral was short, no one came,
Preacher ran quick to catch the Game.
Here she lies in her best gray gown,
lying beneath a dying town.
Laughter runs short when you're in the grave,
God is not dead, yet no one's saved.
Meanwhile, Old Bessie lies in the ground
where all of life will soon be found.

# Excerpt From a Wasted Life

God bless you, child - come walk with me today.
I've grown old, my youthfulness has turned gray;
I see in your eyes a bit of my past,
in your innocence the moment can last.
Child, my grandson, don't grow old like me
letting life go by without time to see
there is more to life than working for pay,
from time to time you've got to get away.
Love your children, don't let them grow alone;
your father had to grow up on his own.
Now he is bitter, not caring for life;
worst of all, he takes it out on his wife.
Your mother, she is a precious woman;
she keeps it all in, and does what she can.
I take the blame for their falling apart:
child, when you grow you can make a new start.
Remember your grandpa, foolishly old;
he did not know life was worth more than gold.

# There's a Man

There's a man standing outside,
inside, trying to get out.
Let him in.

Out of time, out of mind,
he's inside his own head.
Bring him out, let him in.

He's going way too far.
Let him out, bring him in.

This world is not his,
his world is not this.
Let him in.

# Laura

Laura wakes from her dreams
sits up in bed and stares into the night.
Laura looks at the man lying beside her
and wonders what she's doing here.

> Laura is sunshine
> and fresh winter's snow.
> Laura is all things,
> a moonbeam
> with nowhere to go.

Laura, your world is not for you.
You need wider spaces to find the real you.
Laura, you're wasting your life away here.
You need a playground to harbor your games.

He wakes to an empty bed.
Laura is gone.
She's on to new things.
She's got to move on.

> Laura is confusion,
> an empty hole.
> She's lightning, she's fire.
> She's nothing that's real.

Laura, you're heading for death's open door.
Nothing in this life will satisfy you.
Laura, if only I knew a way
to make you happy, and if only you'd stay.

# The Old Mill Stream

By the old mill stream
there I lost my dream
a hundred years ago
when love was just for show.

She was a spring romance
I asked her to the Dance;
swirling to a waltzing tune
the months rolled by all too soon.

Then the winter came,
love was not a game.
We were forever tied
until her love just died.

The waters rose
as her love froze;
it was the old mill stream
that washed away my dream.

# File It Under Mistake

File it under mistake
and move along.
Don't look back on past missteps,
a new relationship waits at the next turn.

Words of wisdom she lived by;
working well for her,
but leaving a trail of broken dreams
for those left behind.

# The Jacket Preacher

The day the jacket preacher came to town
pockets opened wide.
Salvation for just pennies a day,
silver tongued deviltry,
a passion for poetic lines,
the jacket preacher lined his soul.

# Infinity Man

On an oval track.
He keeps running.
Looking to place some distance
from the starting line.

# Living On The Border

Living on the Border,
waiting to cross the line.
Guns on either side
ready to explode.

Living on the Border,
waiting for someone to take a step.
Tensions split on both sides
ready to explode.

# Message on the Phone Machine

The message on the phone machine
was your way of breaking clean.
The voice rewinds a thousand times,
still you never change your mind.
I'm left with this broken dream
and the message on the phone machine.

# Widow

The rap on the door tore into my heart;
nothing had to be said, I saw it in his face.
The newest widow, wife of Badge 323:
someone walks the streets, one less bullet in his gun.

# Glimpses

Carousels,
ice cream cones,
a stolen kiss beneath
the shade of an old elm tree.

Crises of nations,
guns at fire,
dank, dark trenches,
and a picture of you.

Coming home,
parades, banners,
sparklers ablaze.
A bit of rice,
a threshold,
a child radiant
in an ivory gown.

Laughing children,
carousels,
an open embrace on a
new porch swing.

Rocking chairs,
ice cream cones.
Gentle walks,
a stolen kiss beneath
the shade of an old elm tree.

# A Barroom Scene

His world was caving in on him;
it was something he could not comprehend.
He knew that he had done wrong,
he knew that it was a sin.
But in desperation, deep inside
he knew that he was not about to die.

He shot one round into the air,
a second into a friend.
With the third he cared no more,
he shot two more into the law.

The captain said, "This cannot go on."
He ordered out two extra squads.
And as the streets were being cleared,
the confusion served to make him scared.

He shot once more into the crowd;
his words were short, but his gun spoke loud.
He shot wildly into the street,
then he rose up as if to speak.

But, alas, no words did come:
the police had him in their sites,
three shots went through - out went the lights.

He fell upon the barroom floor;
the police came rushing in.
They listened closely for his dying words:
He took a breath, looked out in space,
he could not find a friendly face.

His lips trembled as he spoke,
and before his life faded away
he spoke right out, "I know my limit -
Give me another drink."

# Death Comes To Visit

Quietly he sits in his long glass window.
Patiently he waits for the knock on the door.
"Where is he? Where has he gone?
It's not like him to be so long."
The door opens, slowly creaking,
and the floorboards squeak as he slowly comes creeping.
There he is. It's about time.
You've finally arrived after all these years.
Slowly it leaves, closing the door,
and silently he lies, dead on the floor.

# Death of a common man

" …but common people never really die
    they just sort of slip away
    disappear into the shade
and the world continues on its way
and he thinks that it might be nice to stay
and take a part in the role of the day"

" …but common people can't really die
    they just kind of fade away
and disappear into the morning mist
the one that late rising people will
most certainly miss fade away.

# The Legend of Ganamel

## I
*Ganamel is Born*

Legends sometimes told
on a wintry autumn night
fade into the forests
where wood nymphs
begin their song.

Legends sometimes grow
in the magic of the night.
In the morning's glow
a figure is seen on the hill,
a legend's born anew.

## II
*A Legend Begins*

Somewhere in time
a woman's scream is heard.
Out from the mists of yesterday
Ganamel's cry is raised:
'Today begins the dream.'

A sword against the sun,
a battle easily won.
Victory still tastes sweet;
Ganamel turns to face a new day.
A verse is added to the song.

## III
### *A Legend is Made*

Out of nowhere
a trumpet sounds.
Too close, too soon;
time is never on his side,
the one battle he cannot win.

Ganamel faces the storm,
rages at the dimming light.
One more task to fulfill,
Ganamel enters the stream.
The final note is played.

## IV
### *The Legend of Ganamel*

Legends sometimes told
on a wintry autumn night
fade into the forests
where wood nymphs
begin their song.

Legends sometimes grow
in the magic of the night.
In the morning's glow
a figure is seen on the hill,
a legend's born anew.

# Southern Night

I remember Southern Night,
how we talked about our plight;
how the rain kept coming down,
as the tears inscribed your frown.

I remember Southern Night,
we sat subdued by candlelight.
The sky itself seemed to cry,
as we talked about goodbye.

I'll always remember Southern Night,
though a lot's replaced the site.
They say time heals, maybe it does;
I still mourn a place that never was.

# Trapped in Summer

She battled against the winter,
and never met her fall.
Summer fling held her memory.
Skip through spring,
return to the sun.

She never faced the harshness,
never knew the dawn.
Never felt the pain on her face,
and never grew.

# The Game

There was no one to play the game,
so they asked me to come along.
Tag was never my specialty,
I was always a step behind.

There was no time to explain the rules,
I was 'it', so I went along.
When I tired, I looked for a base to hide,
but there were no islands, only the road ahead.

Some have stopped playing,
by their choice or by the law.
I'm still looking for a way off;
endlessly running, always a step behind.

# The Voyage

The ship set sail from Tanmark Bay;
strong wind blowing, the voyage underway.
Into the night, toward the unknown;
by new morning's light, the reasons were shown.

A battle fought, a battle won;
new direction, follow an eastern sun.
The ship set sail toward Tanmark Bay:
Port - Destiny, it somehow ran astray.

# Joe's Problem

It was Joe's problem,
we all looked away.
A broken life
in a shattered home,
no one came to play.

It was Joe's problem,
no one else would care.
An empty dream
on a burnt out mind,
no one else was there.

It was Joe's problem,
the rest of us couldn't see:
when it all comes down
and all hope is gone
there's only you and me.

# Down in Kenilworth

Down in Kenilworth
Ryland's had a second birth.
Sally walks a lonely hall,
her baby cries, Rick slams the wall.
Old man Neely feels the pain again,
last week he fell, laid there 3 days.

All we do is cry,
heave a lonely sigh.
Life they say goes on.
How long, we pray.
How long?

Kenilworth has known better days,
forgotten by time, life's moved away.
We stay behind, try to get along;
looking to the end is all we have.
It all sounds so sad.

All we do is cry,
heave a lonely sigh.
Life they say goes on.
How long, we pray.
Does anyone hear our prayers?

# (Another) Southern Night

Southern night
in a southern jail.
The old man
wouldn't make my bail.
Plenty of time
for a restless mind
to sort through
a life of crime.

It seemed so long ago,
one small child
so eager to grow,
he found his father's gun;
one shot later
no longer a favorite son.

Lonely life
in a lonely town.
A loveless soul
will bring you down.

# An Empty

She walked into an empty breeze,
in and out of leafless trees.
A past she had is lost in time;
a broken heart, a verseless rhyme.

She entered the year in winter's embrace,
a dreamer still of summer's grace.
Days of sun are far ahead;
tonight's cold sheets, an empty bed.

# The Last Lie

The last lie
broke the chain
of hopelessly hoping.
I am free.
The last lie
has been spoken.

# Him

She sings me a song,
I fall for the tune.
But the words aren't mine alone;
somewhere out there someone
hums the same tune.

# Tendrils

She danced along tendrils
of winged thoughtless flight.
A dangled songbird slighted
by the time.

I wonder,
wonder at design.
No reason for laughter,
beyond life to decide.

She lies across tendrils
of softness ill defined.
A mangled snowflake melted
by the time.

# How the Plague Destroyed Many a Fine Day in the Park

He never escaped the draft,
they always caught him hiding in the rain.
A box he had to filter out the sun,
a bleak device worn with each curse of pain.

She danced across everyone's darkness,
casting and breaking spells of lesser dreams.
The gift was hers to bring forth laughter,
caressing and mending broken tortured seams.

Movements of planets and crashing of worlds
bring great changes, for bad or good.
He once heard her footsteps, if only …
Some defenses last longer than they should.

# Samantha

Samantha
lady of the blue night
      lost for all times.

Lady
silver and wings
      always flying away.

Samantha
blue hoping that
      the stars still shine.

# When The Leaves Fall Down

When the leaves fall down
we may not be here.
Grandma cries a bit,
but she hides the tears.
The mountains where she grew
giving way to modern days.
Soon John and me
will be on our way.

In her younger years
her world was clear.
All she could see
was all she'd be.

It was all they'd need,
together, it seemed to stay.
No one told them then
it would change.

John died before
the coming of the second war.
Grandma was left alone
to her children raise.
But she never complained,
she'd hide the pain.
She never knew
it would change.

When the leaves fall down
we may not be here.
Soon John and me
will be on our way.

# Ride On

The march has begun,
forward they ride to the challenge.
Hearts inflamed,
morning sky in red.
Forget tomorrow,
forget it may never be.
Ride on.

First encounter;
someone wins,
someone's gone.
Second time,
winners don't survive.
The mounts won't care.
Ride on.

# The Danger of Living in the Neutral Zone

Strayed too far from the real world;
calamities abound.
Peace is all, yet it thrives not;
the danger of living in the neutral zone.

Escape an illusion in place of time;
buffers all around.
The only escape a determined mind;
stayed too long in the neutral zone.

# On The Road (Ballad of a Truck Driver)

Driving all night on this lonely highway
I want to rest, stretch my legs.
But I've still a long way to go;
oh, to be home with you.

Miles and miles of empty skyline -
radio's busted, it's a cold November.
Trucking is exciting, it's an occupation;
roads may connect town to town
but they also separate me from you.

Come on heater, don't fail me now -
San Jose's only a few hours away.
Got to get there,
don't know why;
one place is as bad as another
without you to share it with.

Here at last -
but I still can't stop.
Gotta get a room,
got to find a phone:

"Yes dear, it's me
I'm here and I'm fine.
Be home in a week
but for only a day."

Got my run for the next day all set,
which leaves me the night - to forget.
A list of numbers, which one to call:

    "Mary Ellen, it's Jim
    I'm back in town."

A quick shower before she comes round,
or perhaps it should wait
til after she's gone.

It's the road that does it to you;
it wears down your strength.
Endless highways
make one lonely.
Someday I'll quit this job -
I may drive off a cliff.

Driving to nowhere
24 hours a day
makes one crazy.
It may give freedom,
but takes away purpose.

I'll be driving this truck
til the day I die
heading for - but never reaching
the sky.

# The Obscure Magician

The obscure magician
sat in the darkness,
applying his trade of
magic rhyming words
silently.

Pulling dreams out of a hat,
linking solid chains together,
the obscure magician
weaved his spells for himself
alone.

The obscure magician,
with his magic rhyming words,
world-renowned only in his mind.
His red-flamed spirit
followed him to the
grave.

# When The Revolution Came

I thought I heard you calling
before the cannon fire began.
I was looking for you
when the revolution came.

Was that you laughing
in the gently falling rain,
or was it my imagination
looking through the pain?

Guns are overwhelming,
the only color now is red.
Someone wrote a letter
saying you were dead.

I thought I heard you calling
before the cannon fire began.
I was looking for you
when the revolution came.

# Tuesday Morning Paper

The paper said
it was in the head.
The red of my carpet
didn't care.

I don't know why
Mondays always bring me down:
sunshine or rain
Mondays always bring me down.

Too many loud noises
spin 'round the brain;
so many choices –
they're all the same.

I don't know why
Mondays always bring me down:
perfume or chains
Mondays always bring me down.

And the man said
plead insanity,
better locked up than dead.
Caviar & wine or bread & butter,
it's all the same to me.
I don't know why
Mondays always bring me down.

# Nowhere Left To Go

They took it to the danger zone
to find out where the thrills had gone.
But no matter how they tried
still they could not hide
from the truth lying inside.
There's nothing that can be done
once the love has moved on along.

# The Circle

Pressed against the night,
the flower bids goodbye.
We're all against the wall,
inside, about to fall.
Newborn child starts to cry,
the world will be all right.

# Bad Week

Wednesday she read the news,
by Friday she was gone.
They say Sunday is a day for prayer,
but then Monday comes along.
Tuesday was the day of tragedy,
by Thursday a decision had been made.
Come Saturday, a time to seek forgiveness.
They say Sunday is a day for prayer.

# Failed Attempts

She stepped out of her solitude
to catch a rising sun.
She thought she heard the thunder
before her world came undone.

He had a brief encounter
with a girl he almost knew.
He never saw the lightning
until the night drove through.

They tried to find a reason
for not being alone.
They lived in an illusion
until the truth was shown.

# Silence on the Hill

There is a quietness
up on the hill today.
They've gone and buried
my sister Mae.

She would play up there
when she was a child –
running and yelling
so free and so wild.

She never changed
as adulthood came.
Suitors tried to win her love,
she refused to play their game.

It was on that hill
where with other girls she'd run
someone decided to be the judge
with the barrel of his gun.

Now there is sadness
up on that hill.
What fear can't conquer
it seeks to kill.

# Summer's End

Sun's light
begins to fade.
Two porch chairs,
a glass of lemonade.

The ice is melting,
mosquitoes search for blood;
the wind blows easy,
no one hears the thud.

The ice is melted.
Evening has come.
One chair's been empty –
now he joins his love.

# Gettysburg

Not a word was heard
from Gettysburg.
The train pulled out
with no mail onboard,
the whistle did not blow.

We tried listening
for the whispering of ghosts.
Not a song was played
on that judgment day,
the messengers had left town.

There yet may be
ghosts to be found.
Somewhere under the ground
are voices to be let out
in Gettysburg.

# This House

This house …
This house used to laugh;
oh, how we bathed in the laughter.

The children …
It was the children
holding together a foundation
cracked,
cracked below the surface,
lying in wait for a future unseen.

This house
held the dream.
Too many waking hours have passed,
the kids have moved along.
Their houses hold the laughter,
but do the cracks await their time?

# Florence Nightingale

She broke out of silence,
answering the cry within.
Mending without cutting,
each seam gently born anew.
She healed every hurt,
leaving only one hole
when silently she slipped away.

# Contrasts

She painted the sky with her dreams,
he locked himself in with his schemes.
His was a world he could not own,
hers – opportunities yet shown.

# Another Song

Since last July
I've noticed things;
subtle changes
in the love you bring.

Since last July
our lives have turned;
what once was suspected
is now confirmed.

I read the letters
on that summer's day,
of another's passion
many miles away.

Since last July
I've noticed things;
too late I hear the meaning
in the song you sing.

# Marathon Man

He keeps running.
From the man who gave him life
to a God who offered hope.
To a woman who offered family missing
from the guilt tearing him up inside.
He keeps running.

From the God he thought abandoned
from the family that might have been.
To a religion without foundation,
a role that he can't play.
He keeps running.

He keeps running.
From any ties to anchor sanity
to holes of depression
too deep to cover him.
He keeps running.

He keeps running.
Along circular paths
back to the man who set him to flight
toward an unknown destination.
He keeps running.

He keeps running
though he knows the road must end.
He keeps running
toward that which must be.

He keeps running.

# Children of the Dance

We played on the hill,
children of the dance.
On the ground below
the grown-ups waged their wars;
scarring each piece of earth,
hearing only the roar of guns.

Untouched by all the hate
we weaved among the flowers;
laughing at the fools below,
such a crazy show.

Little did we know
someday we'd have to climb down.

# Down Lonely Pathways

He walks alone
down lonely pathways
searching for some way
to break on through.

Hiding in shadows
lurk unhealthy memories
of what cannot be,
though he wants it to.

The waking day
passes quickly away.
He's lost in time
hoping to find
some peace of mind
that he lost at home.

# Yesterday's Smiles

She dwells in yesterday's smiles;
refuses the gloom of present day time.
Morning, she gives thanks for the night:
evening she plays over again.

She never enters the storm,
stays in yesterday's calm;
she's still, she hasn't moved on.

# Leila at Four

Leila speaks of mysteries;
of treasure hunts and honeybees,
of a summer blue and a golden fall –
she sees the wonder in it all.

When Leila starts she does not stop;
she likes to run and loves to hop.
She makes the most of each new day,
there's more to do so she cannot stay.

Leila is a wondrous child;
sometimes sweet, sometimes wild.
While I'd love to hold her here with me
Leila is a girl who must run free.

# So Gentle

Flowers always seem to fall
so gentle in the rain.
Laughter brings the sunshine
and ends the pain.

Somewhere in the mirror
there lives an unfilled life.
There inside the cabinet
she seeks to ease her strife.

Flowers fall so gentle,
but they always die.
Laughter covers the moment,
still we always cry.

# Scared

The telephone rings,
you're afraid to answer
'cause you think the voice
on the other end's not her.

You stay awake all night,
you're on your guard.
You never know in what dream
you might find her.

You wear your smile
inside your coat,
protecting it from the cold.
Morning sun never
penetrates inside.

You are scared,
you are alone.

# Regret

She dines in regal splendor
on the carcasses she helped destroy.
She claims no responsibility
for lives that mattered less than hers.

She rides with pure abandon
through the bodies left behind.
She lives with no compassion
for those beneath her gaze.

Somewhere beyond her view
walks the one she could not kill.
He weeps with full remorse
for the woman he helped create.

# The Ebb and Flow

He was living for the new world order
until he met the mailman's daughter.
She delivered him from death and sin,
then sent him on his way again.

He began looking for another way,
hoping to find something to say.
He fell in love with a fragile soul
bringing him closer to his goal.

By the time she let him go
he believed the world would know
some days are kind, some are not,
but we've got to deal with what we've got.

He was living for some kind of change,
a way perhaps to rearrange
the ebb and flow of each new day,
just a chance that love might stay.

# Once A Hobo ...

It's been many long years
since I've heard a freight train's call.
The road stands silent,
I don't hear the campfire's song.

The only sound today
is the rocker's creak
on the crowded porch
of this senior home.

Still I listen
as I rock along
waiting for the day
when I hear the freight train's call.

# A Simple Tune

It was a simple tune
she loved to play.
He could listen
every night and day
trying to find words
for her melodies.
But nothing he said
put her mind at ease.

Complications
were not her thing.
He couldn't bear
to not hear her sing.
Over and over
both day and night
he struggled
to make the words sound right.

He heard her play her guitar
through the lonely wall.
His only desire
was to give her it all.
He could not accept
as he toiled away
it was a simple tune
she loved to play.

# Emerald

She shines from south of the border,
a vision in green, a signalman's daughter.
She says she'll be here by winter,
so he waits with longing to greet her.

Red nights, gray days pass in succession.
Sun's light fades in regression.
There may be no warning
of the Emerald Girl's dawning.

Someday, though, when all is done
she'll prove to be the only one.
He'll wait for her – however long.
There is no escape from her siren song.

# Lilacs and Lilies

She loves lilacs and lilies,
but daffodils make her cry.
No one gives her roses,
she has no room for them in her heart.

Tulips the color of tangerines
grow along her garden wall.
No one steps inside,
she has no time for outside pleasures.

She still lives in one single day,
the one where she said goodbye.
She remembers the bouquets of yellow
covering the box of wood.

She loves lilacs and lilies,
but daffodils make her cry.

# She Lived on the Hill

She lived on the hill.
She spent her nights by the water's edge
watching the lights of the passing ships,
dreaming of places she'd never see.
She watched the lights at night.

Daytime found her home again
walking from room to room,
searching for the right things to wear
on her coming voyage.

Nighttime found her out again
by the water's edge,
counting each passing ship,
watching the lights.

Daylight would come too soon
back in her lonely home,
roaming from room to room.
She could find no rest.
She lived on the hill.

# Love's Seeker

Pardon me sir, but I was your King.
I once stood upon the hill.
But then I looked down,
someone stole my crown
and I'm looking for it still,
though it doesn't mean a thing.

If for a moment you would hear my tale
I will not hold you for long.
There was a time when love was all,
upon the future Queen I'd call.
Along the way something went wrong.
It took fragile love to make a kingdom fail.

Now I'm a seeker, bearing his load.
Perhaps someone I encounter will hold the key
to finding the path to follow
that may someday allow
the crown to be restored to me.
Until then I will walk this lonely road.

# Tomorrow

She thinks about Tomorrow,
wondering what tomorrow
might bring.
She tries to block the sorrow
as she looks around to borrow
what might have been her diamond ring.

Another day goes by.
She cries.
Then she thinks about Tomorrow,
wondering what tomorrow
might bring.

# (Still Singing) Her Song

It was good while it lasted, but it didn't last long.
She moved on to a different song.
I tried for another hit like the one before,
but the magic wasn't there anymore.
So I spend my nights in the local bars
playing happy tunes to mask the scars.
No matter what I sing they just want to hear
that one love song that brought us near.
I sing it every night hoping to win her back –
that special melody that all others lack.

# Fifteen Days of Rain

Sixteen years a fighter,
he gave his all inside the ring.
But when it came to her
he had nothing left to bring.
Now trying to escape his pain
he drives through fifteen days of rain.

Behind a plastic smile
lay the bruises she kept inside,
yet knowing all the while
her tears she could not hide.
Finally letting go her shame
she cried out fifteen days of rain.

All throughout his career
He basked in each new victory.
He had nothing to fear
except letting her go free.
Unable to accept the blame
he rides through fifteen days of rain.

# He Loved the Night

He loved the night,
he lived for the darkness.
As the stars filled the sky
he found peace at last.

Daylight brought chaos,
sunshine exposed the scars.
The hurt could not be hidden
from the brightness of the day.

He loved the night,
he awaited the dark.
Only in the solitude
could he reveal his heart.

# Downward Spiral

She was in a downward spiral,
looking for a friend.
Twirling, spinning, turning,
reaching toward the end.

Somewhere past a boundary
someone heard her cry.
Hoping, praying, searching,
but neve asking why.

They were bound together, falling
in tandem freefall flight.
Twisting, fighting, failing,
seeking out the light.

# Miss McCready

I've grown so weary
of Miss McCready
telling me things I already know.

She doesn't seem to understand
life isn't always as planned.
It's better sometimes
        to ride the wave
than to hide inside one's cave.

I've grown so weary
of Miss McCready
always telling me no.

# Last Night

Last night
the sun was setting on a tropical paradise.
Last night
I heard the rumblings and tried to set things aright.

You were swimming in a pale blue ocean,
light was dancing off your silhouette.
Musicians were playing with wild abandon
as the singer serenaded the breeze.

Last night
was the perfect combination of sorrow and splendid bliss.
Last night
I heard you breathing as you disappeared into the night.

You were smiling as you heard the music,
water beaded off with every move.
A cold wind swept away our love
as the singer held you with every note.

Last night
the moon was rising on an island set apart.
Last night
I heard the music that put an end to my heart.

# Exercise in Fours and Eights

There was nothing wrong with the night,
but they kept searching for the light.
Until at last it came in sight
they continued to hold on tight.

Some think it's all about the test –
how does one get to be the best?
Some try in vain to find some rest
until they lose all interest.

There could be better days ahead
walking the path where others led.
They chose to hide away instead
seeking cover under their bed.

Some hold that there's a better way.
They might be wrong, but who can say?
Staking all hope on a new day
is the place where they need to stay.

# The Last Scar

Sometimes you go too far
and leave a scar
that doesn't heal.
You seem to realize,
but then you cauterize
anything you feel.

I wish you'd see
what it does to me.
Or perhaps you know.
We can find a way
you always say.
I think I have to go.

# Not Even 9 a.m.

It's not even 9 a.m.
and I've already been down to your grave.
I know that you're not there.
You've moved on to God alone knows where.

Still, I can't help thinking about better times
and the life that we once shared.
Now there's nothing left to save
but these thoughts that won't go away.

It's not normal, I must admit,
to hold such a strong sense of dread
when I look upon the clock on the wall
and realize it's not even 9 a.m.

# An Answer Came

In a morning fog
a voice was heard
rising out of a sleeping world;
in a whisper sweet
as a summer's day,
honeysuckle
and a sparkling ray
of sunshine;
no hiding place
from a message told,
no cover dark,
no secret held
from the searching.

From a distant shore
an answer came
dark as night,
a cloud of rain;
rough not mild,
weak yet strong,
the searching found
what it was looking for.

In a distant time
not far away
what makes sense now
may not be that way.
What we hear may save our lives
if we only have ears
to let our senses guide.

# She Sang

She sang songs of faith
well into the night.
She sang words of grace
that floated through my walls.

I saw her often
as she passed by in the halls.
I never knew her name:
we were just a quick hello.

But she exuded sunshine
in the smile she always wore.
She could make me happy,
if only for a while.

She sang songs of faith
well into the night.
And even in my darkness
she could bring the light.

# My Story
# (A Hobo's Lament)

Will you tell my story?
Will you tell it well?
Will you tell my story,
will you let it swell
to soaring heights
with new delights
around each bend?
Will you tell my story
and let it never end?
Will you tell my story
and let it live again?
Will you tell my story?

Will you sing my song
long after I've been gone?
Will you sing my song,
let it breathe on?
Will you sing it out,
tell the world about
the loves, the laughter
forever after?
Will you sing my song
so the myth goes on?
Will you sing my song?

Will you tell my tale?
Please, share it well –
the truths, the lies
the sad, sad goodbyes.
Will you tell my tale
so that it doesn't die;
perhaps bring back the glory?
Will you tell my story?

# Epilogue

… and the hobo's left town for good

CPSIA information can be obtained
at www.ICGtesting.com
Printed in the USA
BVHW031046120419
545356BV00005B/33/P